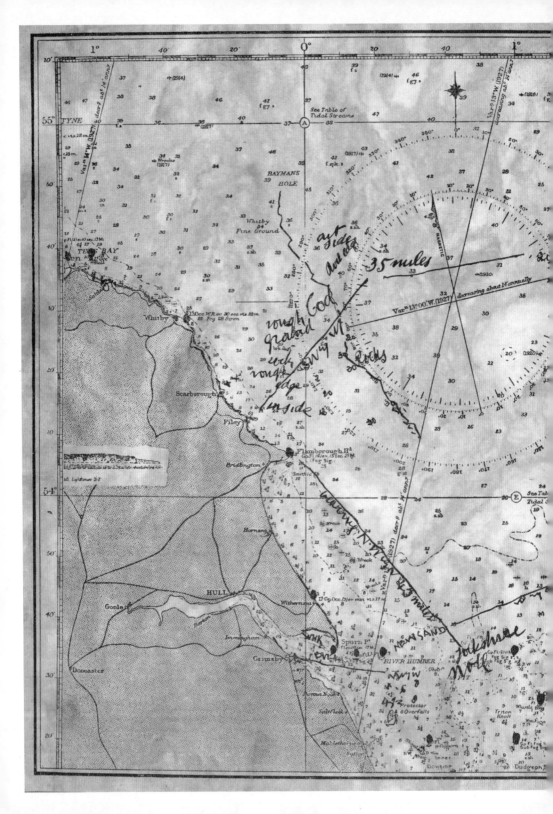

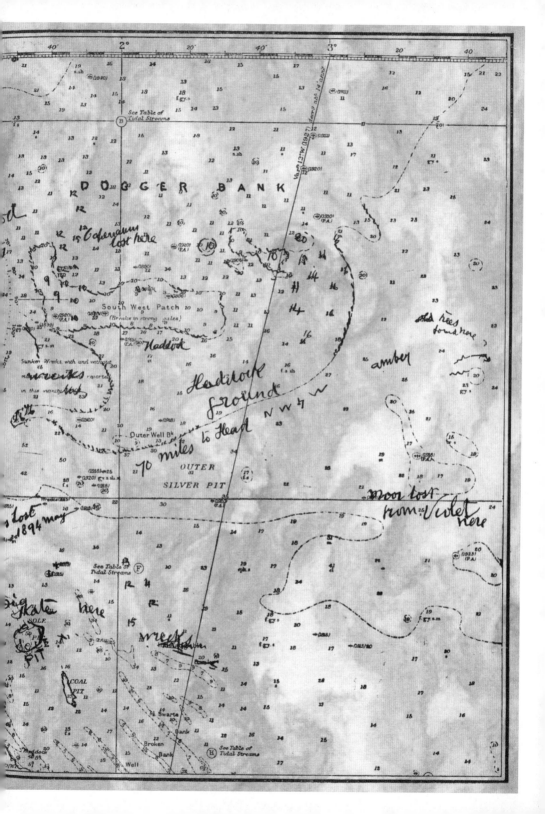

SCARBOROUGH HARBOUR, 1859

SAIL AND OAR

*One hundred drawings of
Yorkshire's North Sea Fishery
before the advent of steam*

by
ERNEST DADE

with a Preface by PETER F ANSON
and a Foreword by FRANK WHEELER

Lodestar Books

First published 1933 by J M Dent & Sons, London
This edition published 2013 by
Lodestar Books
71 Boveney Road, London, SE23 3NL, United Kingdom

www.lodestarbooks.com

A CIP catalogue record for this book
is available from the British Library

ISBN 978-1-907206-23-8

Typeset by Lodestar Books in Equity

Printed in Spain by Graphy Cems, Navarra

All papers used by Lodestar Books
are sourced responsibly

To the memory of the men who sailed and worked in these
craft (may the deep sea, where many of them now
sleep, rock them gently to the end of time)
I dedicate this little book of pictures

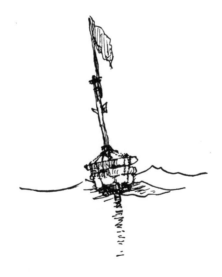

CONTENTS

PREFACE

To ANY ONE WHO IS INTERESTED in the sea and ships Mr. Ernest Dade's drawings of Yorkshire fishing boats will prove an irresistible attraction. Moreover they possess a unique value to the student of the maritime history of Britain, for they form a permanent record of a phase of our nautical annals which has now passed away for ever, due to the introduction of steam- and motor-driven vessels in the fishing industry. Any one who has taken the trouble to search for pictorial representations of the obsolete craft of our coasts will understand what I mean, and they will agree with me in saying that Yorkshire is lucky to have such a capable historian of her splendid seafaring sons and the marvellous little craft in which they sailed. If only other countries and fishing districts had been so fortunate; but alas! it is now too late.

Mr. Dade has known the Yorkshire coast for more than half a century, and most of his life has been spent among the fisherfolk between the Tees and the Humber. There is no living artist who possesses such an intimate knowledge of both the men themselves or of the boats in which they worked.

Many a happy hour have I spent browsing among Mr. Dade's vast collection of old sketch-books from which this selection of drawings has been made, and I rejoice to think that others will now share the pleasure I have often enjoyed, for the sketches possess that rare quality that is only to be found when actually done on the spot without the aid of the camera, which, useful as it is for ensuring accuracy of detail, so often tends to kill the lifelike character of a drawing.

To myself these drawings possess a special interest, for they help to recall days, nearly forty years ago, when, as a boy, I used to try—very ineffectually—to sketch these same fishing boats at Scarborough, Whitby and Robin Hood's Bay. In imagination I can re-picture the fleets of Scottish 'Zulus' and 'Fifies', packed tight like sardines in Scarborough harbour, and whose masts suggested nothing else so much as a forest of trees. I can still see the gaily painted cobles with their brown sails entering or leaving the port; can hear the rough tones of the

Yorkshire fishermen mingling with the softer tones of the Gaelic-speaking lassies from the Highlands, who stood at their barrels gutting the herring—yes! and can even smell the very fish itself as it lay rotting in the hot sunshine on those August mornings while as a seven-year-old boy I wandered around the quays of that fascinating old harbour.

No maritime library will be complete without a copy of this volume on its shelves, for the Yorkshire fishing coble and the Yorkshire smack of the past century were among the finest examples of English sea-going craft ever devised, and none more fitted for the rugged coast to which they belonged or for the stormy seas on which they used to sail.

PETER F. ANSON

THE SHORE, NORTHFLEET, KENT,
Easter 1933

FOREWORD

THIS IS THE FISHERMAN'S LIFE of the North Sea on the Dogger Bank which lies about seventy miles E.N.E. of Flamborough Head, and the Silver Pits which are some miles farther south.

Fifty years ago there were no steam drifters or trawlers, no motors for the cobles or engines for the capstans. The work was all done in sailing craft. There were large fleets of sailing trawlers which were called smacks; the drifters and line-fishing vessels we called yawls; the smallest boats were the cobles, a type peculiar to this coast, and were used along the shore for catching crabs, lobsters, etc., and also for long-lining. Everything was done by sail or oar. Well I remember the long heavy pulls to land in calms with a heavy load of fish, the weary tramps round and round the capstan, carrying sail dangerously in gales of wind to get to market with the catch.

These pictures show all this and are true in every way. Mr. Ernest Dade lived the life, knew the men, and sailed in the various craft he draws so well. It is a record of things passed away. The conditions at sea now are absolutely different. Steam and the internal combustion engine have changed everything, lightened the heavy labour and changed the work. There is plenty of hard work still in the trawlers, drifters and cobles, but the sail and oar have gone for ever.

Frank Wheeler. Fisherman

FILEY
20 December 1932

LIST OF DRAWINGS

SAIL AND OAR

Smacks men 1890

SMACK'S CREW ASHORE

The smack's men were always apprenticed to the owner when boys and when
ashore lived in his house. They worked in the same smack for years.

19

A Trawler Shooting her Gear

This could only be done in a smart breeze so that the net stretched out behind the beam, otherwise it got entangled and would not 'fish' properly.

SMACKS AT SEA

In the old days there were small fleets of sailing trawlers at sea. About every three or four days all the fish was put aboard one fast-sailing trawler and taken to market.

23

Smacksmen Taking the Crew off a Sinking Ship
in the North Sea

These smacks (trawlers) were called the 'lifeboats' of the North Sea. Forty years
ago there were three or four hundred of them at sea. They saved scores of lives;
they would stick to a sinking ship until they had taken off every soul.

Trawler at Sea in a Gale

A trawler stopped at sea during a gale under very short sail, then when the weather got better began fishing again. Calm was much more feared by the old sailing smacks than gales.

SMACKS LEAVING HARBOUR

Trawlers were towed out to sea if there was a tug,
but often had to work out under sail.

AN OLD SMACK OF THE 1870S

The first smacks were very small and had only one mast;
some of them were lengthened and had another mast added.

Lengthening a Smack

The old smacks of the 1870s were one-masted and were found to be too short. They were cut in two and a piece put in the middle. This doubled their tonnage. Although all the gear was used the trawl was simply made larger.

A Lengthened Smack

After lengthening, a mizen-mast was added.

Return of a North Sea Fishing Fleet

The old smacks brought a very powerful odour with them when they returned after six or eight weeks at sea. They could be smelt some miles away.

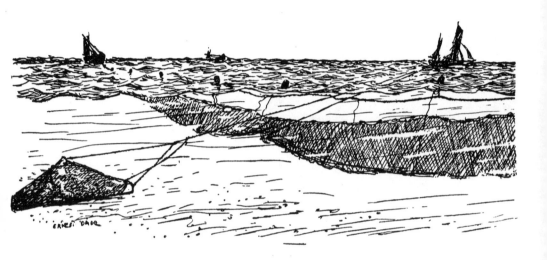

Trawler Cutting Through a Fleet of Herring Nets

When trawling (dragging a net along the bottom) was first introduced in the
North Sea about 1870 there was great opposition from the net and line fishermen.
The drift-net men said the trawlers cut through their nets, and the line men said
the same. This would of course be a night scene. The trawler would naturally
show no lights; the only lights visible would be the drifter's fishing lights. There
seems to be some confusion between a trawler and a drifter–this shows the two
different methods of fishing.

39

THE SMACKSMAN'S STROKE

The smacksman had a lot of pulling to do before steam and the motor came into use. He developed a very curious stroke, in his big high-sided boats, sometimes loaded with heavy boxes of fish.

SMACKSMEN GOING OFF IN THEIR BOAT

The smacks would sail a long way off and give the crews ashore
a long pull to catch them.

Trawlers on the Dogger

Sometimes they were six or eight weeks at sea. The new-comers
were always welcome, bringing letters, messages,
and fresh provisions from home.

THE SMACK

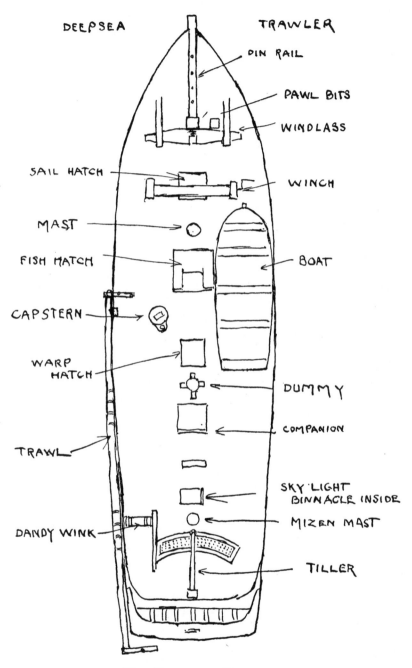

DEEPSEA   TRAWLER

DIN RAIL

PAWL BITS

WINDLASS

SAIL HATCH   WINCH

MAST

FISH HATCH   BOAT

CAPSTERN

WARP HATCH

DUMMY

COMPANION

TRAWL

SKY LIGHT
BINNACLE INSIDE

DANDY WINK   MIZEN MAST

TILLER

THE DECK OF A SMACK

ERNEST. DADE

THE FILEY YAWL 'WILLIAM CLOWES'
BUILT IN 1856; LUGGER RIGGED

In the eighteen-forties and fifties, when the yawls were first built,
there was no trawling; all fish was caught by hook and line in various ways.
The herring in drift nets.

ERNEST·DADE

THE 'WILLIAM CLOWES' CHANGED TO GAFF RIG IN 1870

The old yawls were changed to gaff rig for handiness.
They did not sail so well and were not so picturesque.

51

THE YAWL 'WILLIAM CLOWES' DOUBLED IN 1885

A new skin was built over the old clincher,
which made them much stronger and so lasted longer.

THE YAWL 'WILLIAM CLOWES'

Bought for a club-house by the Scarborough Sailing Club, 1908;
broken up, 1921.

THE CABIN OF A YAWL

The cabins were kept as dark as possible so the men could sleep in the daytime.
There were six berths, but behind the ladder was a large one going right up into
the counter, called the 'hullock', in which four or five boys could sleep.

THE DECK-HOUSE BUILT ON THE 'WILLIAM CLOWES'
BY THE SCARBOROUGH SAILING CLUB

The old yawl-men often came in to have a look at
the different room in their old boat.

Yawls Before the Wind

The Dogger Bank was about seventy-five miles from Flamborough Head,
a few hours' sail; but in calm days—

BAD WEATHER ON THE DOGGER

The water was very shallow on parts of the Dogger Bank
and the sea broke dangerously in gales.

Yawls Going to Sea

The yawls would sail off a dozen or so at a time,
but in a few hours were out of sight of each other.

THE SUMMER FLEET OFF TO THE DOGGER

The summer brought out all the big sails.
Calm was the enemy of the sailing fleets.

HAULING LINES ON THE DOGGER

A long and heavy job. Several miles of lines and thousands of hooks had to be
pulled in and the fish taken off.

YAWLS CARRYING ON TO GET TO MARKET WITH THEIR FISH

Sail was carried as long as possible, to save a tide or land the fish.

71

The Weary Tramp Round and Round the Capstan

The capstan hands were often just picked up at the pier-end for the job. They were sometimes made to partly undress so they could run round easier. It was killing work; worse than the treadmill.

ERNEST DADE

Drift-net Fishing on the Dogger

In the summer fishing the yawls had to catch their own bait. Nets of small mesh
were used from the cobles. They caught very small herring. These were never
sold, only used as bait; but they were very good to eat.

WASHING DOWN

After every trip the fish-room boards were brought on deck
and well scrubbed.

Landing Herrings by Ferry Boat

A favourite way of landing herrings.
The yawl was just anchored and the herrings put into a shore boat.

A Calm

Sometimes the yawls would be becalmed within a few miles of port.
Then commenced the heartbreaking job of pulling a heavy boat and perhaps a
ton of fish eight or ten miles. The man on the rowing thoft pulled a pair of oars,
two men in the main thoft one each, and the steersman pushed one.

81

LIFE ON THE DOGGER

At times the Dogger was quite a lively place, at others perfectly solitary.

ERNEST·DADE

Taking Ice Aboard the Yawls

Ice was carried on trips that were to last longer than three days.

FISHING ON THE DOGGER

A huge dim shape would suddenly come out of the mist. The old sailing ships
were quite silent. The men in the coble had to pull for their lives.

CLEARING THE LINES ON BOARD THE YAWL

This was a long and tiresome job,
and it was done by the owner of the lines himself.

Towing a Loaded Coble

The steam trawlers sometimes gave a loaded coble a tow. It was difficult and dangerous; they were always towed stern first. The trawler didn't stop; the coble had a rope ready which was thrown to the trawler; it passed through a hole in the coble's stern, and the men held on—it was never made fast.

LINES IN THE 'COAL-PIT'

This was very deep water. Large skate and halibut were caught.

The Artist At Work

It was a most interesting and picturesque sight seeing the nets hauled—
generally about daybreak, but lasting some hours.

A CALM

If not more than a mile or so away they would tow the yawl to harbour,
helped by two big sweeps on board.

The Yawl 'Brothers' SH33
Landing Herrings on Filey Beach

This yawl, built in 1840, was one of the first of this type. Before that date they were very small, 'two-ended' (bow and stern the same) boats. The new ones were able to carry and fish a great many more nets and lines.

BOYS FEEDING GULLS FROM THE STERN OF A YAWL

In the summer a lot of boys went to sea in the yawls—quite small boys, ten or eleven years old—just to get used to the sea.

YAWLS RUNNING FOR SHELTER IN A GALE

Gales were sudden and violent in the autumn in the North Sea.

DRIFT-NET FISHING FOR BAIT ON THE DOGGER

The nets were very light, with a small mesh,
sometimes quite on the top of the water.

THE YAWL

HERRING DRIFTER AND LONG LINE FISHER

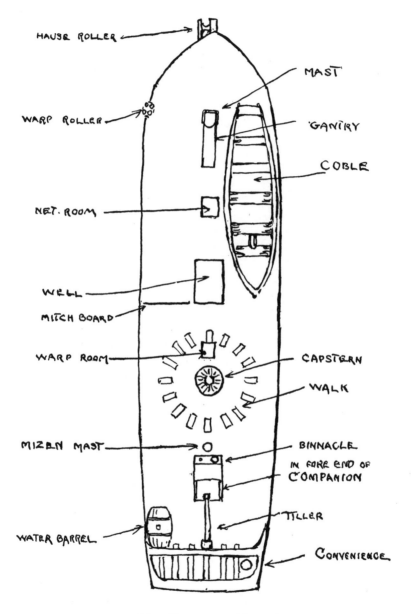

THE DECK OF A YAWL

LIFEBOAT UNDER SAIL AND OAR

Sail was used in certain lifeboats, but only as an auxiliary.

ERNEST DADE

THE LIGHTHOUSE

Beginning a voyage under sail. Forty years ago scores of beautiful schooners, brigs, and barques came from Norway and Sweden to the north-east coast with timber. In a passenger steamer from Hull to Stockholm at the present day not a single sail was seen, only a smudge of smoke the whole passage.

111

Whitby in Herring Time

All the smoke-houses going. In the eighteen-eighties the yawls and large cobles
landed their herrings at the smoke-houses fresh. They were smoked at once
and made the tasty kipper we knew years ago, very different to what we get now
under that name—salt herrings dyed!

113

ERNEST·DADE

A DUTCH BOMSCHUIT ON THE BEACH AT SCARBOROUGH

These Dutch boats were real drifters. They managed to sail to the
Shetlands, where they lowered their masts and sails and 'drifted'.
They always drifted south, fishing all the time,
salting and barreling up the herrings until they were full.

Fécamp Herring Drifter

These were very large, fine boats and had a numerous crew.
Crew going aboard.

A Lifeboat Rescue Under Oars

There are very few rowing lifeboats left; all motors now.

CALM SUMMER MORNING

Herring craft making for harbour under sail and oar. It was a weary job pulling
these big, heavy boats to harbour, perhaps seven or eight miles. No wonder they
preferred gales to calms.

A Long Pull on a Calm Morning out of the Harbour

The crab-pots were left perhaps five or six miles from the harbour;
this distance had to be pulled.

HERRING COBLES RUNNING TO HARBOUR IN A GALE

No wonder they preferred this to calms.

THE BARMSKIN

Used when hauling lines and pots; there were no buttons or anything to catch.

CUTTING UP BAIT FOR CRAB-POTS, WHITBY HARBOUR

The sea-birds always come for their share.

THE COBLE

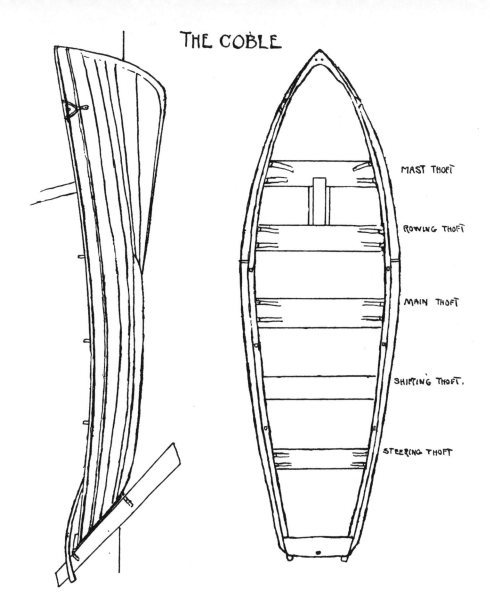

MAST THOFT

ROWING THOFT

MAIN THOFT

SHIFTING THOFT.

STEERING THOFT

WHITBY. ROBIN HOODS BAY SCARBOROUGH FILEY FLAMBOROUGH

THE COBLE

The Lobster Catchers, Filey Brigg

The deep water near the rocks are always good places for lobsters, but there is always the danger of the pots being destroyed if a gale gets up.

An Old Crab Fisherman

The old crab-catchers grew a bit like crabs themselves!

GRAMPUS OR BLOW-FISH

About twenty to thirty feet long, they are always near the shoals of herring.
These were rather alarming if they came to the surface near a boat. The water
was covered with oil when they were about, and they had an awful smell.

The Pleasure Coble

She had no fishing gear and very little ballast; everything cleared away to make
room for passengers.

LOOKING FOR THE CRAB-POT BUOY

After a gale the buoy which marked where the crab-pots were was often moved
by the heavy sea and very difficult to find.

BRINGING CRABS ASHORE

ROBIN HOOD'S BAY CRABBER

One of the best crab-grounds on the north-east coast.

THE HELPERS

These men were always about, to help get the boats ashore.

Coble Running Before the Wind in a Smart Breeze

MAKING FAST THE BOWLINE

ERNEST DADE

FISHING COBLE GETTING UNDER WAY

One man will often work a coble with several lines,
with the assistance of a boy; generally his son.

153

FILEY FISHERMAN COMING ASHORE WITH HIS LINE

Each line was about ninety yards long, with a hook at every
fathom. Each man provided his own line, and cleared and
baited it.

Cobles Tacking in to Land

In strong off-shore winds it was difficult and dangerous
getting hold of the land again.

Long Lines on the Cod-ground

The larger cobles carried a dinghy, called a 'corfe' (calf); it was a cross between an ordinary boat and a coble. Three heavy men would get into one, although only about ten feet long, haul a mile or more of lines and take in perhaps a ton of fish.

SAIL AND OAR

A coble in a light wind would row very easy,
but it became a heavy pull if far away.

161

Rowing and Sailing

The coble could be rowed very easily.
Sometimes the ballast was thrown out in a calm.

CLEARING LINES ASHORE

Each man cleared and baited his own lines.
The smaller boats did the work ashore.

ERNEST. DADE

FISHING COBLE GOING OFF IN A SMART BREEZE

The coble was a fine sailing craft, but required an expert to handle her.

167

At Filey the Cobles are Pulled Up
on Wheels by Horses

The old horses got very clever at this, going into the sea right up to the boat
and turning exactly at the right time so the traces could be hooked on,
and then all pulled together.

169

Staithes Herring Drifter

These were the largest cobles used for rowing and sailing; some of them were thirty-five feet. It was very heavy work pulling in them.

COBLES LANDING ON THE BEACH AT STAITHES

At Staithes the cobles were pulled ashore by hand. The oars were used for
skids, the loom being made very heavy and big for that purpose. Everybody
helped—men, women and children.

OLD CRABBERS LANDING

The old men would keep on crabbing until they could hardly get into their
boats, the crab-pots being quite close to the harbour.

175

ROBIN HOOD'S BAY

At Robin Hood's Bay the cobles are hauled up on wheels by hand.

HERRING COBLE GOING TO SEA

179

FISHING COBLES

As soon as anything like a breeze came,
the coble men dropped their oars and set sail.

181

Herring Cobles Going to Sea Under Sail and Oar

At Whitby there were a lot of these big cobles. In the summer the herrings
come very close to the shore. The shoals can be seen from the piers.
Quantities of herrings are landed and made at once into kippers,
without being salted.

The Steersman in a Calm

He generally pushed an oar.

The North Landing, Flamborough

The cobles were pulled up by a steam-engine.

The South Landing, Flamborough

There are two coble landings at Flamborough Head, one on the north and
one on the south. The village is equidistant between the two, so the men
can use the one most suitable, according to the weather. The cobles are
hauled up by horses.

Breton Fishermen Ashore at Scarborough

French fishermen occasionally land at Scarborough. They are always
interested in our boats, and years ago used to buy quantities of clay pipes.

Herring Fleet Going To Sea

On a summer evening the herring fleet going to sea made a fine sight.
Many different boats and rigs came to the north-east coast.

PENZANCE LUGGER

Many of these craft came to the North Sea in summer for the herring fishing.

195

The Scotch Herring Fleet Arrives at Scarborough

The Scotch herring fleet arrived about September. They came in hundreds and filled up the harbours for a time.

SCOTCH LUGGERS TURNING TO WINDWARD

These big luggers were fine weatherly craft, but the sail had to be lowered
and shifted round the mast every tack; in short tacks the tack of the sail was
brought aft to the mast, the sail had to be reduced, and was not so effective.

A Very Effective Sail-plan from Lowestoft

Lowestoft Herring Drifters

This was the last word in sailing craft for fishing —
huge topsails and spinnakers like those of yachts.

CORNISH FISHERMEN AT SCARBOROUGH

Fleets of Cornish herring craft came north years ago. They were good
fishermen, but it was a stormy coast compared with Cornwall.

Scotch Herring Luggers Under Sail and Oar

THE PILOT

PENZANCE LUGGERS AT SCARBOROUGH

211

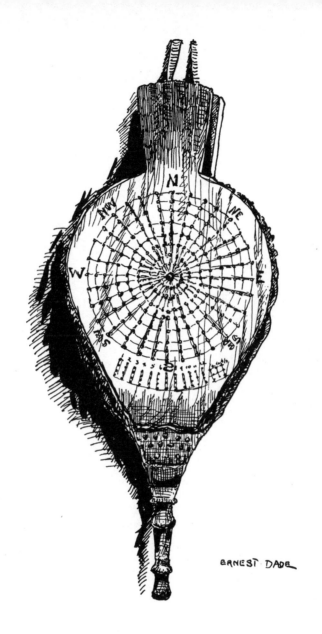

ERNEST DADE

TRAVERSE BOARD CARVED ON A PAIR OF BELLOWS
IN USE ON BOARD A PENZANCE LUGGER IN 1887

The points of the compass are clearly inscribed, and in the line of each point are
eight small holes; a wooden peg was placed in the hole corresponding with the
course sailed every half-hour of the watch.

Scotch Herring Lugger

These fine big craft played a great part in the autumn herring fishing.

SCOTCH HERRING LUGGERS

The Restored Bridlington Sailing Coble
THREE BROTHERS

The Bridlington Sailing Coble Preservation Society
www.bridsailingcoble.org.uk

THE COBLE IS A VERY ANCIENT FORM OF BOAT, and was most probably brought to our North East coast by the Angles from Germany, and Danes who came to establish fishing settlements from the Humber Estuary northwards. The design was supposed to be based on that of Viking longships and certainly it combines excellent seagoing characteristics with easy beaching and control in shallow water. The name itself has been used for more than 1,000 years and variations are found in Celtic (ceubal) and Breton (caubal) and the name is used in the Lindisfarne Gospels. As might be expected, the pronunciation varies. On the Yorkshire Coast it is "cobble" whilst farther north in Northumberland it becomes "co-ble," using the long "o." In general form the boat has remained very much the same. Certainly those early settlers would recognise *Three Brothers*, which the Bridlington Harbour Commissioners bought and restored, as still being of the same design as the cobles they used so successfully. They would be able to sail, row and beach her too, all of which were necessary capabilities.

The villages and fishing towns on the Yorkshire Coast began their histories as settlements which were very independent and isolated, and through many generations their families formed a significant coastal fishing industry which only began to lose its importance after World War II. The sailing coble was the foundation of the industry, and the background of these sturdy fishing families. Until about 1920 there were a great many of these boats. Mostly they were built locally, and generally the builders used no plans, but relied with great skill on hand, eye and experience. Their tools were the adze, hammer, chisel, and maul. It is said of Angus Hopwood, who built boats at the rear of his house in North Marine Road at Flamborough, that he dismantled an old coble on the beach, noted the parts, and went home to become a famous coble builder. His iron work was done by Wiles in Tower

Street, Flamborough—a family with several generations of blacksmith craftsmen. Here in Bridlington two men still thought of with admiration were Baker and Percy Siddall. They had a workshop in Bow Street, which is still owned by Mr Percy Siddall's family. It was there that they built *Three Brothers* in 1912.

She is now the last of these sailing cobles built in the town, and is rather special in design, having less 'sheer' than usual—sheer being the rising curves of the lines fore and aft—and so was much flatter, to allow beam trawling as well as passenger carrying. More sheer would be called for if it was planned to use more sail. In appearance the boats were wedge shaped at the bow, and flat bottomed towards the stern, which made it easier to use them from the beaches. They had two bilge keels called drafts. These are like deep sledge runners made of ironshod oak, and they run from the stem, or about the forward third of the boat, back to the stern. The forefoot or backward continuation of the prow is also iron shod, and on the beach the boat rests on these three iron lengths so that the hull itself is well clear of the ground. The ram plank is the continuing central keel from the end of the stem forward to the overhang of the square stern aft, and coble lengths are often given as the length of this ram. In *Three Brothers*, the ram length is 27ft and the overall length 40ft.

The need for fast easy beaching combined with what is known as weatherliness at sea is met by oars, and a very deep rudder. This is long and narrow, and pivots by means of an iron rod or pintle, which is pushed into a hole in an iron plate on the stern. It is important when beaching or taking up a harbour berth that the rudder can be unshipped rapidly and without fail. The fishermen became extraordinarily skilful in handling these boats—and after sweeping in under sail the final position against a pier would be achieved by oar or a 30ft boathook. Then the unshipped long rudder would be used as a boarding or crossing plank to other cobles. The forward part of the boat was decked over to give a "cuddy" with some 4ft to 5ft of headroom and this provided some shelter, and housed the small stove and supplies. Cobles were clinker built—that is, the hull was shaped by ribs or timbers, and overlapping planks—they had a very shallow draught, and were propelled by oar and dipping lug sail.

The smaller details in the design tended to vary in the different communities as each had their own idea of proper beam, sheer, and tumblehome. The Siddall

brothers used more ribs or timbers than others, and some variations in length were allowed. The building cost of *Three Brothers*, excluding the sails and iron work, was £75 (cost would be £4950 in 2013). The iron work was done by Tom Rowntree, and this would include the rudder gudgeons, the pintles, stem irons, the keel and draft irons. The total building time was about six months.

In 1914, a 40ft coble like *Three Brothers* cost £90 (£5940) and its sails £25 (£1650). These were made locally by Raddings, although many of the cobles were rigged with sails from Broadmeadows of Burnham-on-Crouch. The mast set forward would be 30ft to 36ft tall, stepped in extra timbers in the frame, and it was braced by lateral backstays, and a forward jib tie. There was usually a bowsprit, sometimes up to 28ft long, and this could be retracted. Some of the boats also used a mizzen mast set towards the stern for trawling or even racing. Two rudders would be carried—a long one of 10ft to 12ft which had a hardwood head on a pine body—and a short tiller (6ft) on a short rudder, all of hardwood. The rudders were always unshipped in the harbour.

The main sail was made of about 110 square yards of cotton duck with a varying number of reef points, and sets of jib sails were also carried. These ranged from large 90 square yards to the storm jibs around 15 square yards. The mizzen sail, when used, was much lighter, being made of calico or union silk, and the responsibility for handling this sail rested on the ship's "lad."

The cobles were the maids of all harbour work, and they thrived in great numbers. Between 20 and 30 could be seen drawn up at the Flamborough North and South Landings, and a similar number in Bridlington Harbour. They were used for herring netting, crabbing, and long-line fishing when a very small coble would be stowed aboard the parent boat, and used under oars to haul the lines. This small boat was called a "calf."

Trawling had its time, and bigger ships coming into the Bay had to be serviced by the cobles with supplies of all kinds, sometimes coal, which was ferried in six or seven-ton loads, and delivered in 5cwt baskets.

Three Brothers is a reminder of the cobles' past, of their importance, and of the part they played in the growth of Bridlington as a sea-side town and resort. She is pictured in the summer of 2013 following a major refurbishment. She remains engineless, and negotiates the harbour with the aid of a side tow.

Publisher's Note

We are grateful to the Bridlington Sailing Coble Preservation Society for our Postscript on the coble *Three Brothers*, a fine example of England's North Sea fishery heritage being preserved for later generations to appreciate; and to Mike Wilson for our use of his photographs.

On p137 is a slight mystery. The name Grampus was applied colloquially to the Orca, of length twenty to thirty feet, and to Risso's Dolphin, about ten to fourteen feet long. The Orca (or 'Killer Whale') is suggested by the caption's mention of the animal's length; but adult Orcas are unmistakable with their upright dorsal fin six feet or more in height, which Dade does not draw here. However juvenile Orcas can be confused, at a distance, with Risso's Dolphin. It is uncertain which animal was known as 'blow-fish'—perhaps any class of dolphin was. Both species are commonly seen in the North Sea.

The chart of the Dogger Bank on pages 2-3, with its annotations by a local fisherman, formed the endpapers to the first edition in 1933.